History's Travellers and Explorers

Philip Ardagh

Illustrated by Chris Mould

Belitha Press

First published in Great Britain in 1996 by
Belitha Press Limited
London House, Great Eastern Wharf
Parkgate Road, London SW11 4NQ

ISBN 185561 518 5

Printed in Hong Kong

British Library Cataloguing in Publication Data for this book is available from the British Library.

Editor: Maria O'Neill
Designer: Hayley Cove
Consultant: Bryn Hammond

CONTENTS

Introduction 5

Marco Polo 6

Captain Cook 8

Magellan and Drake 10

Isabelle Eberhardt 12

Hernando Cortés 14

Burke and Wills 16

Livingstone and Stanley 18

Amundsen and Scott 20

Ibn Battuta 22

Columbus and Cabot 24

Mary Kingsley 26

World Map 28

Glossary 30

When They Lived 31

Index 32

INTRODUCTION

In most people's minds, an **intrepid** traveller or explorer is usually a white, European man – often with a beard – who discovered somewhere famous and named it after himself or after his **monarch.**

You'll find plenty of people fitting that description in this book, but there are others . . . and beware of the word 'discovered'. It is human nature to claim to be the first person to have seen something or to have gone somewhere. For example, David Livingstone is credited as having discovered the Victoria Falls in 1855, on what is now the Zimbabwe/Zambia border . . . But it seems unlikely that the local people failed to notice the 120-metre-high waterfall until a Scotsman came along and pointed it out to them. But there is no doubt that the travellers in this book were brave and stepped into what was, for them, the unknown.

Words which appear in **bold** can be found in the glossary on page 30.

MARCO POLO

Born in Venice, Italy, in 1254, Marco Polo was certainly an intrepid traveller. It was a short spell in prison that made him famous. He shared a cell with a man named Rustichello and they passed the time by talking about their lives. Polo did most of the talking.

Rustichello was fascinated by his cell-mate's amazing adventures, and decided to write a book about them. The result was *The Travels of Marco Polo*. It contains the first descriptions of the Far East by a European.

Though much of the book was based on truth, some of the so-called facts are a little hard to believe. Polo talked about seeing some very strange creatures. At a time when many Europeans had never set foot out of their home towns, Marco Polo travelled from Venice, via Jerusalem across Persia to China then back, by sea, via Malaya, Sumatra, Sri Lanka, India and the Straits of Hormuz.

Polo started travelling in 1271 when he was only 17 years old, and was 41 when he finally returned home to Venice. He did much of his original travelling with his father and uncle, but – because the book was more about him than about them – few people even remember their names. (They were Niccolo and Maffeo Polo, if you must know.)

Young Marco had the extraordinary honour of becoming a representative of Kublai Khan, the mighty **Mongol** leader of China. He was even sent on a number of important diplomatic missions.

Gunpowder stories

When Marco Polo came home to Venice, he brought with him news of paper money, gunpowder and porcelain vases – all things unheard of in the West until then. He ended up in prison during the war between Venice and Genoa.

CAPTAIN COOK

Captain James Cook wasn't a travel agent. (That was Mr Thomas Cook.) James Cook was an officer in the British Navy. But, unlike most British officers, he didn't come from the upper classes. He was the son of a farm labourer.

Although Cook captained the ship the *Endeavour* in 1768, he really held the lower rank of lieutenant. Following secret orders, he went to Tahiti and New Zealand in 1769 on a scientific mission. He had a spot of bother – involving over 90 **Maori** warriors in canoes – so moved on. In 1770 he was the first European to set foot in Australia. He landed in an **inlet**, which he named 'Botany Bay' after the amazing number of plants that he saw there. (Botany is the science of studying plants.)

Cook went on to lead two further expeditions, the first in 1772 and the second in 1776. In Easter 1774, he reached an island and named it 'Easter Island'. There he saw some incredible carved giant stone heads, some up to 12 metres tall. In 1778, he sailed to Hawaii.

To begin with, Cook and his men were treated like gods by the Hawaiians. But things took a turn for the worse. Cook set sail for home but his ship was damaged in a storm. He returned to Hawaii to carry out vital repairs, but a scuffle broke out with the locals, and Cook was stabbed and died.

Cook improved the lives of ordinary sailors. He took masses of fruit on his voyages, to help beat **scurvy** – the main cause of death for the sailors of the day. He also made his men wash regularly. This may have led to a few raised eyebrows, but it resulted in far healthier crews.

The tattoo tradition

It was Cook's contact with the Mcoris which led to the tradition of sailors having tattoos. Maoris loved tattoos and showed Cook's men how they were done. When the British sailors returned home, the practice spread.

MAGELLAN AND DRAKE

The first expedition to sail around the world was led by a Portuguese man called Ferdinand Magellan. Another term for sailing around the world is 'circumnavigating the globe'. This voyage took from 1519 until 1522. Sadly, Magellan and most of his crew didn't live to finish the whole voyage. Magellan set off from Spain with five ships and 260 men. Only one ship, the *Vittoria*, returned three years later, with a few men on board.

The expedition ran into numerous problems along the way: too little food, dreadful weather, enemy attacks and shipwrecks. Magellan himself was killed in the Philippines during a dispute between local tribal chiefs.

The next circumnavigation of the globe was led by the Englishman, Francis Drake. His expedition took him from 1577 to 1580. His mission was twofold. First, to find out whether a place called Tierra del Fuego was an island or part of an enormous 'undiscovered' continent. Second, Queen Elizabeth the First of England wanted him to come back with plenty of gold and spices . . . even if this did mean a little piracy along the way.

Despite all the bad luck that fate could throw at him, including **mutinies** among his crew, Drake finally reached Tierra del Fuego and was able to confirm that it was actually an island. He returned to England in November 1580.

Knighted on board

Drake was knighted on board his ship by the queen, to become Sir Francis Drake. He was knighted because he'd managed to attack passing Spanish ships and steal plenty of gold and silver from them.

ISABELLE EBERHARDT

Born on the outskirts of Geneva, Switzerland in 1877, Isabelle Eberhardt was the daughter of Nathalie Eberhardt, a Russian noblewoman. She thought that her father was her mother's husband, Paul de Moerder, a general in **Tsar** Alexander's Imperial Guards. What she never knew was that the man she called 'great uncle', Alexander Trophimovsky – an **anarchist** and children's tutor – was in fact her real father.

Isabelle Eberhardt was a remarkable person. In her mid-twenties, she went to North Africa to explore the Sahara Desert on horseback. This was an amazing achievement for a woman in the early 1900s.

If this wasn't amazing enough, she also dressed as an Arab man! Most Arab people she met knew that she was neither Arab, nor a man, but they politely treated her as if they hadn't noticed.

Many of Eberhardt's adventures are recorded in her diaries, written between 1900 and 1903. She became a Muslim and persuaded her mother to convert also. This was why she resented the suggestion that an Arab man who attempted to kill her in 1901 had done so because she was a Christian.

She was so angered by this that she wrote to a French language newspaper arguing that this was not the case. (The French ruled much of North Africa at the time.) Fortunately, the worst she suffered in this mysterious attack was an injured arm which healed – and expulsion from Algeria. She returned to the country when she married an Arab man.

Eberhardt spent several years travelling. She suffered from illness and lack of food and was often very short of money.

What finally killed her, at the age of 27, was being in the wrong place at the wrong time. While visiting the desert on the border between Algeria and Morocco, she was drowned in a freak flash flood. Of all the places a European might expect to drown, a desert must come near the bottom of the list.

HERNANDO CORTÉS

Born in 1485 into a respected Spanish family with plenty of pride but little money, Hernando Cortés had his first adventure at the age of 26. Under the command of a man named Diego Velazquez, he went on a mission to seize what is now Cuba. Cortés ended up mayor of Santiago de Cuba, the capital. He was rich and famous – but he wanted more.

Cortés had heard stories of the Aztec people who lived on the American mainland, and of their gold. In 1519, he led a force of 600 men into what is now Mexico. He entered the city of Tenochtitlan and was thought by many Aztecs to be the god Quetzalcoatl. The Aztec emperor, Montezuma, had other ideas. He played along with the pretence that this traveller was a god, but kept a close eye on him.

Letters home

Despite his ruthless nature and a reputation for being a **conquistador**, Cortés appreciated the beauty of the countries he conquered for Spain. A number of letters he wrote between 1519 and 1526 contain wonderful descriptions of the landscapes he crossed.

Smallpox

The Spanish's greatest weapon was **smallpox**, and other diseases which the sailors carried with them from Europe. The Aztecs caught these terrible diseases and thousands died. It was only a matter of time before the sophisticated Aztec civilization was at an end.

Unfortunately for Montezuma, he didn't watch Cortés closely enough. The Aztec emperor became Cortés' prisoner and was taken to the city of Vera Cruz on the coast.

Meanwhile, back in Tenochtitlan, one of Cortés' men had killed a group of Aztecs at a religious meeting. This upset the Aztecs and things got out of hand.

When Cortés went back, he tried to calm things down by producing their emperor. This was a bad move. The Aztecs had never particularly liked Montezuma and stoned him to death. Cortés and his men were forced out of the city. They laid siege to it and eventually recaptured it in 1521.

Burke and Wills

Burke and Wills took up the challenge of trying to be the first people to cross Australia. Their reason? A cash prize of £10 000 was on offer. And in 1860, £10 000 was a very big prize indeed.

Robert O'Hara Burke, an Irish ex-soldier and Melbourne police inspector, was the leader of one of the largest and most expensive expeditions in Australian history. His navigator and astronomer was William J Wills of the Melbourne **Observatory**.

There were two major problems with the expedition from the word go. First, Burke and his men were unfamiliar with the sort of terrain that they were crossing. Second, none of them had any real experience of being explorers. Both Burke and Wills did, however, have extremely fine beards!

They set off in August 1860 and were dead before the end of 1861. The team was enormous with 23 horse-drawn wagons and 24 camels . . . all travelling at different speeds and causing chaos.

Eventually, Burke, Wills and two other members of the team, Charles Gray and John King, split away from the main group, in an effort to reach the far coast. The main group, under the charge of William Brahe, camped at a place called Cooper's Creek and waited for them there.

Burke, Wills, Gray and King reached the north coast but, on the return journey, bad weather and bad luck led to Charles Gray's death. When the others returned to Cooper's Creek, they found the place deserted and a note from Brahe. He had assumed them all dead and, with food running out, he was leading the main group back home to safety. Instead of trying to meet up with them, Burke, Wills and King decided to go a different way. They got lost in the **outback** and had to eat the last of their camels to stay alive. Giving up, they returned to Cooper's Creek.

It was here that Burke and Wills died. Later, the bodies of Robert Burke and William Wills were taken to Melbourne and given a state funeral.

A helping hand

Charles King was the only survivor from the team that split away from the main group. King survived thanks to some **Aborigine** people who found him and looked after him until he recovered.

LIVINGSTONE AND STANLEY

David Livingstone, born to a poor Scottish family, became a Christian **missionary** in southern Africa in 1840. This was at a time when black African people were being kidnapped and sold as slaves. This horrified Livingstone. He decided to explore and 'open up' as much of central Africa to white Christian missionaries as possible. He hoped that Christianity and **commerce** might, somehow, lead to an end of the slave trade.

In 1841, on the other side of the world, in Wales, John Rowlands was born. After years in a **workhouse**, he ran away to America, where he was adopted by Henry Morton Stanley. He took the man's name.

Livingstone, meanwhile, had discovered the Zambezi River with his wife, Mary, their children and a local guide. From 1854 to 1856, he became the first white European to walk the width of Africa. He returned to Britain a hero.

The Victoria Falls

David Livingstone was the first white person to come face-to-face with the 120-metre-high waterfall on the Zambezi River. He named it the Victoria Falls, in honour of his monarch, Queen Victoria, who had many things and places named after her.

Livingstone returned to Africa in 1866. He made no contact with anyone at home in England for three years. An American newspaper, the *New York Herald*, sent Stanley (formerly Rowlands) to try to find him. Stanley set off from Zanzibar on the east coast of Africa with just under 200 native **porters** and an enormous amount of supplies.

On 10 November 1871, the two men finally met in a village called Ujiji. There, Stanley is said to have spoken the famous words: 'Doctor Livingstone, I presume?' Livingstone was weak and ill but soon recovered. With supplies sent by Stanley, Livingstone went on his last expedition in 1872. He died during this expedition in 1873.

Stanley returned to Africa in 1874 'to complete the work left unfinished . . . by the death of Doctor Livingstone' and set off exploring with a team of over 350 men. As if that wasn't enough, he took 800 men with him on his next expedition in 1887.

AMUNDSEN AND SCOTT

Both Amundsen and Scott died tragically. Amundsen, the Norwegian, came first in the race to the South Pole. But it is the Englishman, Robert Scott, who was given the title 'Scott of the Antarctic' and is remembered as the great explorer. Sometimes history just isn't fair.

Roald Amundsen was planning a trip across the Arctic to the North Pole when he learnt that an American had already reached it. He decided to try for the South Pole instead. Amundsen knew that Scott had already set off on an expedition there in August 1910. He did the 'decent thing' and sent Scott a message to let him know that it had turned into a race.

Scott's expedition included a team of 53 men, horses and scientific equipment. The horses were not used to freezing conditions, and the bulky equipment slowed them down. The clothes Scott and his men wore provided little protection.

Amundsen had proper clothing, dogs and fewer men. On 14 December 1911, he reached the South Pole and raised the Norwegian flag. Scott arrived there – with four of his men – on 18 January 1912. Downhearted, they headed back to their depot, where they had stored food and fuel for a fire. One man died on the way. Back at the depot, the fuel had leaked out. The four men had nothing to keep them warm. Eight months later, a rescue party found their frozen bodies in a tent.

In 1926, Amundsen became the first person to reach both Poles. He was flown over the South Pole in an airship piloted by his friend Umberto Nobile. In 1928, Nobile crashed in the North polar region, and Amundsen went out searching for him. He died in the attempt.

The missing body

There were only three frozen bodies in Scott's tent. The fourth man, Captain Lawrence Oates, had been worried that he might be holding the others back – but he knew they wouldn't leave him there. One evening, he left the tent, saying: 'I'm going now. I may be some time.' He was never seen again.

IBN BATTUTA

Ibn Battuta was a rich Moroccan Muslim who became a seasoned traveller more by circumstances than by design. As a Muslim, he wanted to visit Mecca, the birth place of the prophet Mohammed, so he set off on a **pilgrimage** in 1325.

His travels took him from Morocco, across Egypt, to places such as Jerusalem and Damascus. Battuta soon realized that he loved exploring.

Once in Mecca, he decided to travel further and visited Baghdad in the north. The city lay in ruins. It had been ravaged by the fierce Asian warrior race called the Mongols.

Back in Mecca, Battuta studied law and became a Quadi (a kind of judge).

To cap it all

Battuta's home town of Fez gave its name to an unusual kind of hat. The fez has no brim, and is shaped like a cone with no point. It is usually red with a tassel.

His new-found skill earned him enough money to go travelling again. This time he sailed down the Indian Ocean off the African coast, visiting the towns of Mombasa and Kilwa. He returned to Mecca via the Persian Gulf and the Arabian Peninsula.

But this still wasn't enough for Ibn Battuta. Before long, he was crossing through Afghanistan to India and from there, by sea, to China. He finally made it back to the town of Fez, in Morocco, in 1349.

Did this mark the end of his travelling days? Certainly not. The best was yet to come. In 1352, he crossed the Sahara Desert to explore Mali and to visit Timbuktu, keeping a written record of the places he visited and the people he met. This was at a time when many of the places he explored were unknown to Europeans.

In all, this most intrepid traveller is estimated to have travelled over 120 000 kilometres in his life – further than most of us go today, even with the benefit of the aeroplane.

COLUMBUS AND CABOT

No book about explorers, great or small, would be complete without Christopher Columbus, the man famous for discovering North America.

Of course, many people set foot in America long before Columbus arrived. There were the Native Americans, for example. Originally from Asia, they had walked to America thousands of years earlier, when Asia was joined to America by land and ice.

It is also likely that the Vikings reached America long before Columbus. But it was Columbus who is credited as having 'discovered' the continent in 1492 . . . even though he didn't realize that he'd found it. For the rest of his life, he was convinced that he had reached China!

Buried in chains

Columbus was born in Italy, but his voyage was funded by King Ferdinand and Queen Isabella of Spain. Later, he fell out with the king and queen over his poor treatment of the islanders and Spanish there. In 1498, Columbus was sent back to Spain in chains. The queen forgave him, but Columbus insisted that when he died, he should be buried in chains to remind the world of how he had been treated.

In 1497, another explorer, John Cabot, set out from the port of Bristol in England. John Cabot led this expedition in search of a route to China and landed on the North American continent – in what is now Canada. Unlike Columbus, he was fully aware of the importance of his discovery. This voyage was the original basis for England laying claims to North America.

In Bristol today, there is a statue and tower named after Cabot as a tribute to his voyage of discovery. In fact, John Cabot's real name was Giovanni Caboto and, far from being an English hero, he was, like Columbus, born in Italy . . . but the English paid for his expedition!

MARY KINGSLEY

Mary Kingsley was born in London, England on 13 October 1862. Her brother Charles was born in May 1866. Although not as bright as his sister, he was sent to Cambridge University at great expense and sacrifice to the family. Mary stayed at home.

As with so many Victorian daughters, Kingsley acted as a nurse to her mother when she was ill . . . from 1887 to 1892. Her father, meanwhile, travelled the world as a private physician to rich, aristocratic families. Both her father and mother died in 1892. Within six weeks of her mother's death, Mary Kingsley set off on her travels.

She is most famous for her adventures in West Africa. Kingsley achieved two major 'firsts'. She scaled a hitherto unclimbed face of Mount Cameroon in September 1895. She also canoed down the dangerous rapids of the Ogooué River in July 1895. She wrote about her adventures and claimed to be nicknamed 'Only me' by the black Africans, because she called out 'It's only me' when entering their villages.

Kingsley said that she never wore anything but the ordinary clothes of a Victorian lady, including long skirts. At the time, Europeans would have been outraged by a lady wearing trousers. She even declared that she was once saved from the teeth of a crocodile by the thickness of her 'voluminous skirts'.

The Boer War broke out in South Africa in 1899 and Mary Kingsley went there to be a nurse. She died on 3 June 1900 and was buried at sea off the African coast.

A fish called Kingsley

Mary Kingsley liked to collect rare fish and one species was named after her. This is said to have pleased her greatly. There is no record of the fish's thoughts on the matter.

WORLD MAP AND KEY PLACES

CHINA
Baghdad
Mecca
INDIA
INDIAN OCEAN
PACIFIC OCEAN
Zanzibar
Victoria Falls
AUSTRALIA
Cooper's Creek
Botany Bay
NEW ZEALAND
THE ANTARCTIC

GLOSSARY

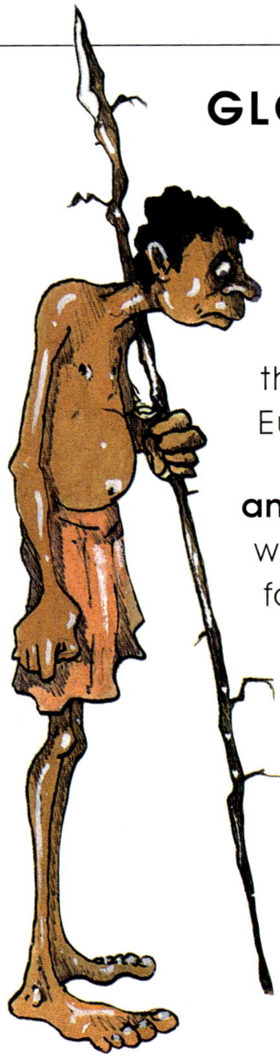

Aborigine: one of the native peoples of Australia who were already living there when the Europeans arrived.

anarchist: person who wants to get rid of all forms of government.

commerce: trade – buying and selling.

conquistador: 16th century Spanish conqueror of the Americas.

inlet: a small bay.

intrepid: brave, daring or bold.

Maori: people already living in New Zealand and the Cook Islands before Europeans settled there.

missionary: a person sent abroad on a religious mission by his or her church.

monarch: a king, queen or ruler who is born into the position.

Mongol: a person from Mongolia, a huge region in central Asia.

mutinies: revolts against those in charge (usually sailors against ships' captains).

observatory: a building with telescopes and equipment for studying the stars.

outback: Australia's remote bush country.

pilgrimage: a journey to worship at a holy place.

porters: people who carry supplies (usually inhabitants of the country).

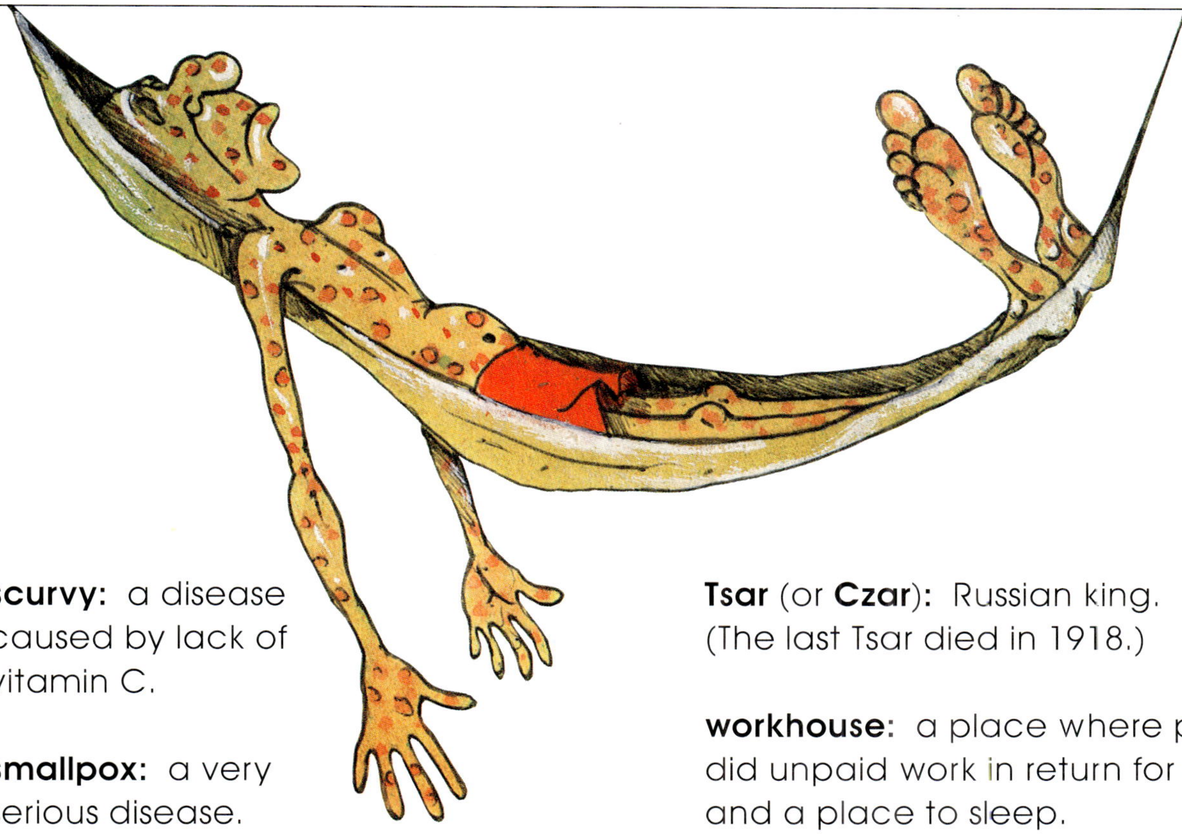

scurvy: a disease caused by lack of vitamin C.

smallpox: a very serious disease.

Tsar (or **Czar**): Russian king. (The last Tsar died in 1918.)

workhouse: a place where people did unpaid work in return for food and a place to sleep.

WHEN THEY LIVED

c1254 – 1324 Marco Polo

1304 – 1377 Ibn Battuta

c1450 – 1498 John Cabot

c1451 – 1506 Christopher Columbus

c1480 – 1521 Ferdinand Magellan

1485 – 1547 Hernando Cortés

c1540 – 1596 Francis Drake

1728 – 1779 James Cook

1813 – 1873 David Livingstone

1820 – 1861 Robert Burke

1834 – 1861 William Wills

1841 – 1904 Henry Morton Stanley

1862 – 1900 Mary Kingsley

1868 – 1912 Robert Falcon Scott

1872 – 1928 Roald Amundsen

1877 – 1904 Isabelle Eberhardt

INDEX

Aborigines 17
Africa 12, 13, 18, 19, 23, 27, 28
Amundsen, Roald 20-21, 31
Antarctic 20, 21, 29
Arabian Peninsula 23
Arctic 20
Asia 24
Australia 8, 16, 17, 29
Aztecs 14, 15

Battuta, Ibn 22-23, 31
Boer War 27
Botany Bay 8
Brahe, William 16, 17
Bristol 25, 28
Burke, Robert O'Hara 16-17, 31

Cabot, John 25, 31
Canada 25
China 7, 23, 24, 25, 29
Columbus, Christopher 24, 31
Cook, Captain James 8-9, 31
Cooper's Creek 16, 17, 29
Cortés, Hernando 14-15, 31
Cuba 14, 28

Damascus 22
Drake, Sir Francis 11, 31

Easter Island 8, 9
Eberhardt, Isabelle 12-13, 31
Elizabeth I, Queen of England 11
Endeavour, The 8

Ferdinand and Isabella, King and Queen of Spain 24
Fez 23, 28

Gray, Charles 17
gunpowder 7

India 7, 23

Jerusalem 7, 22

Kalahari Desert 19
Khan, Kublai 7
King, John 16, 17
Kingsley, Mary 26-27, 31

Livingstone, David 5, 18-19, 31

Magellan, Ferdinand 10, 31
Malaya 7
Mali 23
Maoris 8
Mecca 22, 23, 29
Mexico 14, 28
missionary 18
Mombasa 23
Mongols 22
Montezuma 14, 15
Morocco 13, 22, 23, 28
Mount Cameroon 27, 28
Muslim 13, 22

New Zealand 8, 29
Nobile, Umberto 21
North America 24, 25, 28
North Pole 20

Oates, Captain Lawrence 21
Ogooué River 27

paper money 7
Persia 7
Philippines 10
pilgrimage 22
Polo, Marco 6-7, 31
Rustichello 6

Sahara Desert 12, 23, 28
Santiago 14
Scott, Robert Falcon 20-21, 31
scurvy 9
slaves 18
smallpox 15
South Pole 20, 21
Spain 10, 11, 14, 15, 24, 28
spices 11
Sri Lanka 7
Stanley, Henry Morton 19, 31
Straits of Hormuz 7
Sumatra 7

Tahiti 8
tattoos 9
Tenochtitlan 14, 15, 28
Timbuktu 23
Travels of Marco Polo, The 6, 7

Ujiji 19

Velazquez, Diego 14
Venice 7
Vera Cruz 15
Victoria Falls 5, 19, 29
Victoria, Queen of England 19
Vikings 24
Vittoria, The 10

Wills, William J 16-17, 31

Zambezi River 19
Zanzibar 19